BIG TALK

POEMS FOR FOUR VOICES

PAUL FLEISCHMAN

ILLUSTRATED BY BEPPE GIACOBBE

How to read this book

Get ready: Find three other speakers.

Get set: Pick a color.

Go! Read the words for your color
all the way through the poem.

Green and yellow
read together

Green and yellow
are silent

Everyone reads

Grandma rockin'   **We've just always been the sort who like the quiet evenings here.**

Grandma rockin'   **We've just always been the sort who like the quiet evenings here.**

Clock tick-tockin'   **We've just always been the sort who like the quiet evenings here.**

Clock tick-tockin'   **We've just always been the sort who like the quiet evenings here.**

Orange and purple
are silent

Orange and purple
read together

Hop down to the next group
of four lines without stopping

Helpful hints

Try to speak at the same speed as the others. Watching the other lines and looking ahead on your own will help you know when to come in.

The first poem is the easiest and will get you ready for the second. The second will get you ready for the third.

Want some variety? Try switching with someone. Can't find four readers? Two speakers can manage the book by taking two lines each. Got more than four? Try reading two to a line.

**You're ready to make BIG TALK.
Have some toe-tapping,
tongue-flapping fun!**

Contents

Some folks go to movies

Gunshots, chases, screams of fear

We've never been that kind of folks

Grandma rockin'   We've just always been the

Grandma rockin'   We've just always been the

Clock tick-tockin' We've just always been the

We'd rather stay right here.   Clock tick-tockin' We've just always been the

sort who like the quiet evenings here.   Some folks love the speedway

sort who like the quiet evenings here.   Roarin' engines,

sort who like the quiet evenings here.

sort who like the quiet evenings here.

9

Grindin' gears   Grandma rockin'

                                                                                   Grandma rockin'

          We've never been that kind of folks

                              We'd rather stay right here.

                    Sister hummin'   We've just always been the sort who like

                    Sister hummin'   We've just always been the sort who like

Clock tick-tockin'   Grandpa strummin'   We've just always been the sort who like

Clock tick-tockin'   Grandpa strummin'   We've just always been the sort who like

the quiet evenings here.   Some folks like the opera

the quiet evenings here.   Singers screechin' in your ears

the quiet evenings here.

the quiet evenings here.

                                                  Grandma rockin'

                                                  Grandma rockin'

We've never been that kind of folks

                          We'd rather stay right here.

Sister hummin'   Raindrops rappin'

Sister hummin'   Raindrops rappin'

Clock tick-tockin'   Grandpa strummin'   Toes a-tappin'

Clock tick-tockin'   Grandpa strummin'   Toes a-tappin'

We've just always been the sort who like the quiet evenings here.   Some folks like their

We've just always been the sort who like the quiet evenings here.

We've just always been the sort who like the quiet evenings here.

We've just always been the sort who like the quiet evenings here.

12

wrestling

Bones a-breakin', shouts and jeers

We've never been that kind of folks

We'd rather

Grandma rockin'   Sister hummin'

Grandma rockin'   Sister hummin'

Clock tick-tockin'   Grandpa strummin'

stay right here.   Clock tick-tockin'   Grandpa strummin'

Raindrops rappin'   Roof-leak droppin'   We've just always been the

Raindrops rappin'   Roof-leak droppin'   We've just always been the

Toes a-tappin'   Fire a-poppin'   We've just always been the

Toes a-tappin'   Fire a-poppin'   We've just always been the

sort who like the quiet evenings here.   Some folks go out dancin'

sort who like the quiet evenings here.   Band a-blarin', whoops

sort who like the quiet evenings here.

sort who like the quiet evenings here.

Grandma rockin'

and cheers   Grandma rockin'

We've never been that kind of folks

We'd rather stay right here.

Sister hummin'   Raindrops rappin'

Sister hummin'   Raindrops rappin'

Clock tick-tockin'   Grandpa strummin'   Toes a-tappin'

Clock tick-tockin'   Grandpa strummin'   Toes a-tappin'

Roof-leak droppin'   Uncle fiddlin'   We've just always been

Roof-leak droppin'   Uncle fiddlin'   We've just always been

               Fire a-poppin'   Brother whittlin'   We've just always been

               Fire a-poppin'   Brother whittlin'   We've just always been

the sort who like the quiet evenings here.   Living in the city's

the sort who like the quiet evenings here.   Just too loud for

the sort who like the quiet evenings here.

the sort who like the quiet evenings here.

16

Grandma rockin'

country ears   Grandma rockin'

We've never been that kind of folks

We'd rather stay right here.

Sister hummin'   Raindrops rappin'

Sister hummin'   Raindrops rappin'

Clock tick-tockin'   Grandpa strummin'   Toes a-tappin'

Clock tick-tockin'   Grandpa strummin'   Toes a-tappin'

Roof-leak droppin'   Uncle fiddlin'   Crickets chirpin'

Roof-leak droppin'   Uncle fiddlin'   Crickets chirpin'

       Fire a-poppin'   Brother whittlin'

       Fire a-poppin'   Brother whittlin'

       We've just always been the sort who like the tranquil

       We've just always been the sort who like the   soothing

Bullfrogs burpin'   We've just always been the sort who like the   peaceful

Bullfrogs burpin'   We've just always been the sort who like the

   quiet evenings here.

   quiet evenings here.

   quiet evenings here.

placid *quiet* evenings here.

Seventh-Grade

Soap Opera

Brenda calls Gregory

Derek snubs Catherine

Ingrid tells Beverley

Jason eyes Jacqueline

Rick gives his e-mail address to Penelope

Faith invites Gwendolyn

Faith invites Gwendolyn

Faith invites Gwendolyn Chelsea lets Brad read her

Dawn sits with Benjamin Sonya sneaks out of the house, gets her ears

Dawn sits with Benjamin   gets her ears

Dawn sits with Benjamin

answers in history

pierced with Lauren and Lynn,   then bumps into her grandmother   Freddy preens

pierced with Lauren and Lynn,   then bumps into her grandmother

then bumps into her grandmother   Flora plots

then bumps into her grandmother

	Randy pays Nicholas not to tell		Mr. Blair what went wrong
Fletcher pleads	Randy	Nicholas	Mr. Blair
	Randy	Nicholas	Mr. Blair
Frieda pouts	Randy	Nicholas	Mr. Blair

when he helped Jeremy dye his hair

Jeremy

Jeremy   Garrett is grounded

Jeremy   Alison traces the phone call and

                                              Seth finds the note in his Julie sees Jill holding

              Miriam swears that she   Julie sees Jill holding

and threatens to   Julie sees Jill holding

                                                          Julie sees Jill holding

hands with Lance at the dance Jason warns Jennifer

hands with Lance at the dance Sue comforts Melanie

hands with Lance at the dance Mark moves to Michigan

hands with Lance at the dance

Anthony somehow misplaces his saxophone

Kelsey's caught

Kelsey's caught

Sheila stalks Stephanie Kelsey's caught

24

Eric's found eavesdropping

shoplifting Eric's found eavesdropping

shoplifting Eric's found eavesdropping

shoplifting   Valerie's parents bar her from the telephone

Gloria sleepwalks at Emily's sleepover, crosses the street, and walks into the pancake house

at Emily's sleepover, crosses the street, and walks into the pancake house

and walks into the pancake house

and walks into the pancake house

Malcolm flunks   Christopher interviews Pamela for

                    Michael fumes   Christopher   Pamela

            Mona fibs   Christopher   Pamela

                    Marsha faints Christopher   Pamela

the school paper and prints what Vince said about Sylvia

                    Vince   Sylvia

                    Vince   Sylvia

                    Vince   Sylvia   Monica's horoscope says that she

Drew loses hope because Kate makes her mind up

Violet breaks up with Kate makes her mind up

Dana refuses to go to the Kate makes her mind up

Kate makes her mind up

to quit watching soap operas.

to quit watching soap operas.

to quit watching soap operas.

to quit watching soap operas.

27

Come to the window!

She's bringing the platters

The children are chattering

Scooting their

The evening meal is about to begin!

The evening meal is about to begin!

The evening meal is about to begin!   They're mortals,

chairs in   The evening meal is about to begin!   No blessing beforehand?

They're blind as the streams underground

They're blind as the streams underground

remember   Deaf as millstones

Unthinking as stumps

29

They don't know what ghosts know.   What a grace I would speak

They don't know what ghosts know.   What a grace I would speak

They don't know what ghosts know.   What a grace I would speak, what a hymn I would sing

They don't know what ghosts know.   What a grace I would speak, what a hymn I would sing

acclaiming even the unnoticed napkins

                                        How quickly the lad snatches his off the table

To feel just once more   white as sun upon snow

To feel just once more   stiff as bark

To feel   starched

To feel   the weight of proud linen

To savor   To search

To savor its smoothness between thumb and finger   To search

To savor   To search for my mother's invisible stitches

To savor   To search

To open it   What a gift beyond price that would be.

To open it   What a gift beyond price that would be.

To open it   What a gift   that would be.

To open it carefully as a love note   What a gift   that would be.

Do you remember?

Do you remember?

Yes, I remember

See there — the girl has started her salad!   Yes, I remember

A jungle explored by fork   Yes, I remember, I'll always

                    Tints flashing   Yes, I remember, I'll always

                    Tastes crouching Yes, I remember, I'll always

                                        Yes, I remember, I'll always

remember.

remember.   The sharpness

remember.   The deckle-edged lettuce

remember.   The wet crunch of cucumbers, each an oasis

33

Tomatoes sliced up into seed-bearing galleons   The unlikely marriage of oil

of scallions   The unlikely marriage of oil

                                                   The unlikely marriage

                                                   The unlikely marriage

            soother   How well I remember.   The father has picked up a roll!

            soother   How well I remember.

and vinegar   lip-scorcher How well I remember.

and vinegar   lip-scorcher How well I remember.

To hold one, a small treasure chest

Lucky man!   To hold one

Lucky man!   To hold one

To feel it warming your hand like a hearth   To hold one

built of wheat   slowly   start

To open it slowly   start

slowly   To lift back its lid   start

slowly   Then to start when the steam, like a

To feel the fit of a knife in your palm

To feel the fit of a knife in your palm

To feel the fit of a knife in your palm

spirit, flies out   To do battle with butter

brick-hard and defiant   soft and servile   I'm hungry for hunger!

brick-hard and defiant   soft and servile   I'm hungry for hunger!

                    in wintertime   in July.   I'm hungry for hunger!

                    in wintertime   in July.   I'm hungry for hunger!

What rapture, that tug in the stomach

when butter and rolls are close by.

when butter and rolls are close by.

when butter and rolls are close by.

Corn on the cob!   Perfect bliss!

Corn on the cob!   So strange how they hurry

Hot from the pot!   They're mortals

Hot from the pot!

37

To joy in

To joy in

To joy in   misting your spectacles

Remember   To joy in the river of steam rushing past your face

To march down the rows with your eager incisors

heating your cheekbones   To bite into

To bite into

To march down the rows with your eager incisors

sweet as sugar   To leave the cob closely cropped

summer itself, sweet as sugar   thin as a new-shorn sheep

summer itself, sweet as sugar

sweet as sugar

The favorite course of the teeth!

The favorite course of the teeth!

Fresh corn!   The favorite course of the teeth!   What is it he's

Fresh corn!   The favorite course of the teeth!   The father is rising

Baked chicken, still sizzling! Can you still remember? To dine on the scent first

Baked chicken, still sizzling! Can you still remember?

carving? Baked chicken! Can you still remember?

Baked chicken! Can you still remember?

Yes, I remember

The opera's overture Yes, I remember

Meal in miniature Yes, I remember

Yes, I remember To choose from potatoes,

40

surrounding the fowl like a vegetable court

p o t a t o e s

p o t a t o e s, white onions   To detect with

white onions, bright carrots   To detect with

every separate seasoning   Pepper

every separate seasoning   bold rosemary

your tongue every separate seasoning   soft-spoken parsley

your tongue every separate seasoning

41

To dip your spoon into the moat of meat juices   Baked chicken, so worthy

Baked chicken, still sizzling, so worthy

Baked chicken, still sizzling, so worthy

To dip your spoon into the moat of meat juices   Baked chicken, so worthy

of praise.   Impossible!

of praise.   He's standing Impossible!

of praise.   She's standing   Finished so soon?

of praise.   Look there!   Finished so soon?

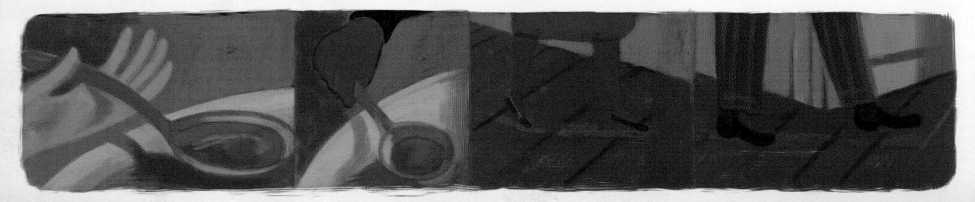

They're all leaving the room!   The fools!   Each meal's a museum to stroll

They're all leaving the room!   The fools!

They're all leaving the room!   They're mortals

They're all leaving the room!   They're mortals

through   To sit at the table, my sisters,

     not sprint   my sisters,

     meant for stopping

     and staring

my brothers, my parents around me   I'm so hungry!

my brothers, my parents around me   I'm so hungry!

my parents, my children around me   I'm so hungry!   the feasting

my parents, my children around me   For that I'm so hungry!   The feasting, the stories

          the feasting   All gone!   Never again

the feasting, the stories   All gone!

the stories, the licking   All gone!   Leaving only remembrance of long ago

the licking, the laughing   All gone!   Leaving only remembrance of long ago

to taste food, to taste family!   But let's come watch tomorrow.

to taste food, to taste family!   But let's come watch tomorrow.

          to taste family!   But let's come watch tomorrow.

          to taste family!   Let's leave this place . . . But let's come watch tomorrow.

44